Bible HIDDEN PICTURE Fun

Activity Book

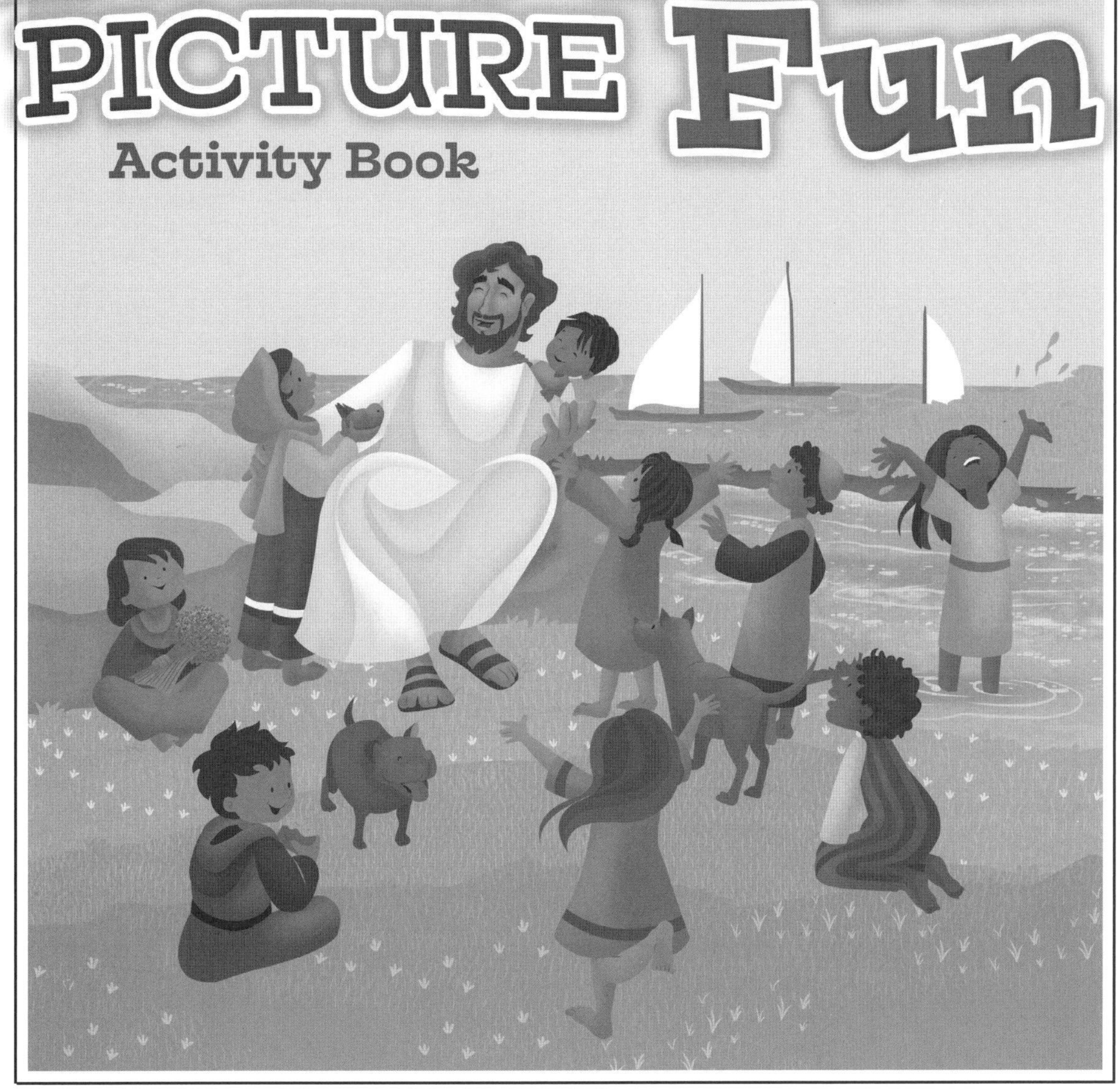

Written by Robin Loisch
Illustrated by Marcela Gomez

3058002100000569

God told Noah He was going to send a flood. He told Noah to build an ark to keep his family and two of every kind of animal safe. When the flood was over, God put a rainbow in the sky and promised never to flood the whole earth again.

Circle the hidden pictures. *(Genesis 6–9:17)*

People were bringing their children to Jesus so He could bless them. The disciples wanted them to go away. Jesus was very upset with the disciples. He said, "Let the little children come to me…for the kingdom of God belongs to such as these."

Circle the hidden pictures. *(Mark 10:13–16)*

Jacob loved his son Joseph the most. He gave Joseph a beautiful robe, and Joseph's brothers were jealous. When Joseph told them about his dreams, his brothers hated him even more. They sold Joseph as a slave to some merchants who took him away to Egypt.

Circle the hidden pictures. ______________________________ *(Genesis 37)*

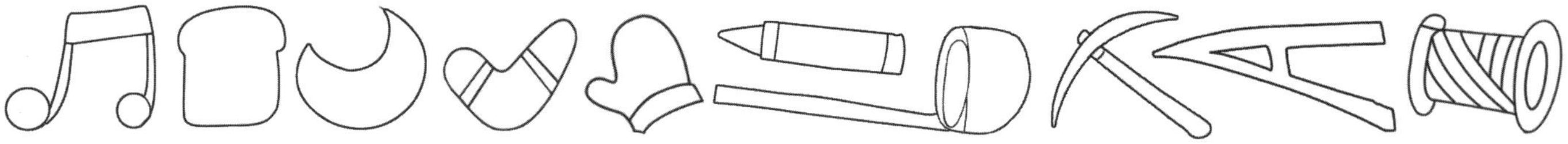

A man's youngest son asked for his inheritance. Then he went away and spent the money foolishly. When he had nothing left, he got a job feeding pigs. He decided to go home and ask to be a servant. When his father saw him, he forgave him and welcomed him home.

Circle the hidden pictures. *(Luke 15:11–32)*

On Mount Sinai, God gave Moses the Ten Commandments, written on two stone tablets. The commandments were God's laws for how the people should live to please and honor God. Moses taught the people everything that God said.

Circle the hidden pictures. ______________________________ *(Exodus 19—20)*

Blind Bartimaeus sat begging beside the road. When he heard Jesus was coming, he shouted, "Have mercy on me!" Jesus asked Bartimaeus what he wanted. "I want to see," he said. Jesus said, "Your faith has healed you." Right away, Bartimaeus could see!

Circle the hidden pictures. *(Mark 10:46–52)*

David's father sent him to check on his brothers in the army. The giant, Goliath, was yelling, and the soldiers were afraid. David said, "I will fight Goliath." He took his sling and five smooth stones. Then he slung a stone, hit the giant on the head, and killed him.

Circle the hidden pictures. ______________________________ *(1 Samuel 17)*

A lame man sat every day by the temple gate called Beautiful. Peter and John heard him begging, and Peter told him they had no money to give him. Then Peter gave the man something better. Taking his hand, Peter helped the man stand, and he was healed!

Circle the hidden pictures. ______________________________ *(Act 3)*

God told Jonah to go to Ninevah to preach. Instead, Jonah got on a ship to run away from God. A terrible storm came, and the sailors threw Jonah overboard. God sent a huge fish to swallow Jonah. When Jonah told God he would obey, the fish spit Jonah onto dry land.

Circle the hidden pictures. *(Jonah 1–4)*

An Ethiopian man was on his way home after worshiping God. He was reading a scroll of the Book of Isaiah. God told Philip to catch up with him. Philip told the man that the scriptures were about Jesus. The man believed and was baptized. Then Philip disappeared.

Circle the hidden pictures. (Act 8:26-40)

Shadrach, Meshach, and Abednego would not worship the king's statue, so he had the men thrown into a fiery furnace. Then the king saw a fourth man who looked like the Son of God in the fire too. God kept the three men safe in the furnace. They did not even smell like smoke.

Circle the hidden pictures. _______________ *(Daniel 3)*

Paul and Silas were beaten and thrown in jail, where they prayed and sang to God. Suddenly, an earthquake came! The jail doors flew open, and the prisoners' chains fell off. When the jailer saw this, he asked how to be saved. Paul and Silas told him about Jesus, and he and his family believed.

Circle the hidden pictures. *(Acts 16:16–40)*

The king did not know Esther was a Jew when he chose her to be queen. An evil man, Haman, tricked the king into ordering the Jews to be killed. Esther risked her life to save her people. When the king realized what Haman had done, Haman was killed, and the Jews were saved.

Circle the hidden pictures. ____________________ *(Esther 2–8)*

Paul was a prisoner on a ship headed to Rome. He warned against sailing any further, but the men wouldn't listen. A terrible storm came, and the ship was about to be torn apart. An angel told Paul what to do. This time the men in charge listened, and everyone on board lived.

Circle the hidden pictures. *(Acts 27)*

 E5108

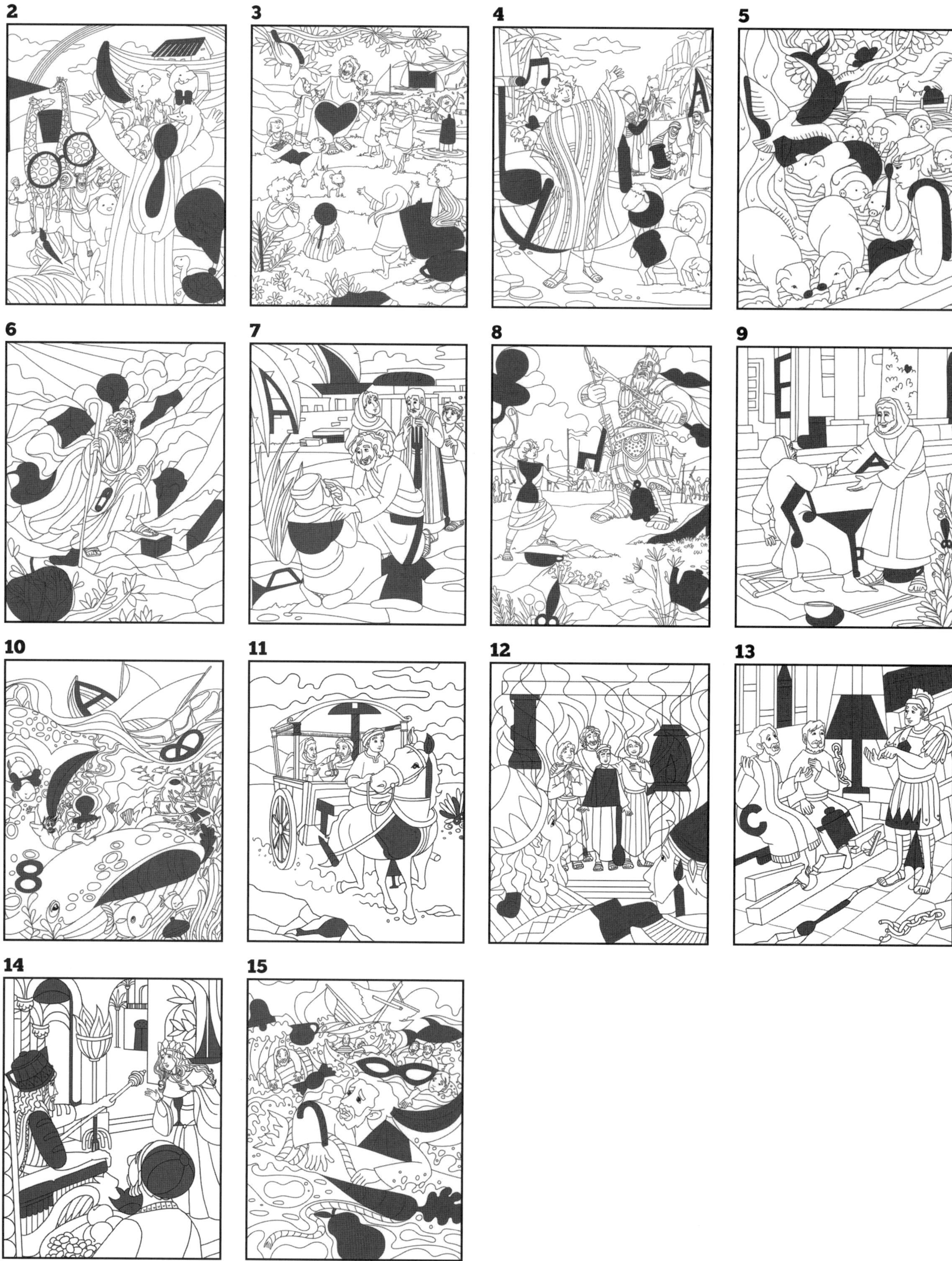
2
3
4
5
6
7
8
9
10
11
12
13
14
15